SANKOFA

Look to Your Past Forgotten Heritage
A Christian Rite of Passage for African-American Males

About the Author

Paula J. Penn-Nabrit, a Columbus, Ohio native, is the second of four children and the eldest of three sisters. She was baptized at the Church of Christ of the Apostolic Faith in 1960 and received the infilling of the Holy Ghost in 1965.

Paula graduated from Columbus School for Girls in 1972 and Wellesley College in 1976. In June of that same year she married the love of her life, Charles Madison "CMadison" Nabrit. In 1977 CMadison encouraged Paula to enroll at The Moritz College of Law at The Ohio State University, her next big adventure.

Although law school was interrupted in 1980 with the birth of twins Charles and Damon. Paula returned to earn her Juris Doctorate in 1981. With law school finished, Paula focused all her attention inward to family. Paula and CMadison gleefully welcomed their final child, son Evan, in 1982.

In 1983 CMadison was working for American Transtech, a wholly owned subsidiary of AT&T, created as a critical component of the divestiture process ordered by the U.S. Justice Department. As a "trailing spouse" Paula was offered a position as a Security Consultant. She was responsible for the review and distribution of all AT&T stocks into the seven newly formed Regional Holding Companies, RHCs, affectionately known as the "Baby Bells."

Paula is the author of several articles and five books including <u>As for Me and My House</u>, <u>Exploring a New Synthesis: Business Ethics & Diversity</u> (An African-American Female Perspective in Essays, Papers and Cases), <u>Morning by Morning: How We Home-Schooled Our African-American Sons to the Ivy</u>

League, <u>The Power of a Virtuous Woman</u>, and <u>Wisdom Traditions</u>. Widowed in 2013, Paula lives in Westerville, OH.

Table of Contents

Receive my instruction, and not silver; and knowledge rather than choice gold. For wisdom is better than rubies; and all the things that may be desired are not to be compared to it. -- Proverbs 8:10-11

Introduction

How to Use this Book

INTRODUCTION

This book is designed primarily as a resource and reference manual for parents and sons to use together. When Charles and Damon, our eldest sons were 12, we decided we wanted to do something to mark their passage from childhood into adolescence, the doorway to their adult lives. We wanted that something to be indicative of the significance of the passage. Most importantly we wanted the "event" to be reflective of their development and their growth as individuals within an ongoing trajectory. All too often milestones in our lives go unnoticed as we scurry from one phase to the next. We felt our sons' upcoming 13th birthday was an excellent opportunity for all of us, individually and collectively to stop, or at least pause, and seriously contemplate what it means to be an adult living in community with others.

It took us almost six months to decide what type of event or occurrence we wanted to see happen. We attended several bar mitzvah ceremonies, researched traditional and contemporary African rites of passage and we borrowed liberally from all of them. In the final analysis however, we decided our sons needed something that bridged their spiritual and intellectual development in a continuum with an analysis of the past, present, and potential future of African-American men. Having decided on the objective and methodology, we devoted the remaining six months to the implementation. Charles and Damon began a rigorous schedule of reading, writing, and discussion of designated scriptures with our Pastor, African scholars, their father and me.

Our intent was to ensure they had a working knowledge of both the history of people of African descent in these United States and of the spiritual strength that ultimately allowed us to survive and prosper. In all honesty it was an arduous six months, fraught with controversy and conflict. The boys felt it was definitely too much work: too much reading of difficult material; too much writing, rewriting and rewriting again; too much analysis and discussion with too many adults. Nevertheless, as is readily apparent in the following pages, the process and the product were both worth the struggle.

We really grew as a family and as parents, the insights we gained of each of our sons, Charles, Damon and their younger brother Evan, watching and waiting in the wings for his turn, those insights proved invaluable.

The following pages contain the actual program of one family's Christian Rite of Passage, in toto, ie., Charles' and Damon's speeches are reprinted as they were written and delivered by them on May 15, 1993. As time consuming and unpleasant as much of the process was, the end results were well worth it to us as parent planners and participants.

Please use this book as a tool as your family works together to determine what kind of "passage" you want your son or your daughter to experience. You may decide the bibliography is too narrowly focused, too academic or too short for your needs. However you choose to structure your adolescent's passage, I am certain it will prove to be a milestone for that child, for your entire family and for the community of individuals involved in your child's life.

Step One: Articulation

The first step was our determination as parents to indelibly mark our sons' passage from childhood to young manhood. CMadison and I forced ourselves to sit down and begin the arduous process of articulating precisely what we expected of our sons. Charles and Damon, our eldest, were fraternal twins. They were young, rapidly maturing African-American males and we wanted our expectations to be as clear as possible. Our hope was that our expectations would help them shape their own.

Part of the rationale for this critical first step was the desire to circumvent what we term the vortex of assumption. All too often consensus of goals, if achieved within the family or community, is not articulated to children moving to adulthood. The existence of such a consensus of goals is not articulated, in fact the existence of goals, simple and complex is neither expressed nor implied. WIthout an expressed or implied articulation of positive goals, a negative space is created. Within this vacuum nonproductive and unhealthy beliefs and behaviors evolve and foster.

We wanted to assure ourselves that we clearly had begun the process of life sustaining goal articulation for our sons. Begun is emphasized as the development and certainly the attainment of goals is an ongoing, highly personal process to be engaged in fully by our sons. Our job, essentially, is to create an environment conducive to their growth and development in that process.

As we began this first step, we were forced to confront both the individual and societal assumptions of what it means to be a "man". First, there is the general, societal assumption of the need or desire to dominate other individuals and Nature herself. And sadly too often that need or desire manifests in forms of physical aggression and violence whether threatened or realized. This is an irrational assumption as neither the need nor the desire to abusively dominate is not an inherent aspect of manhood or masculinity.

A second societal assumption posits external and quantitative validation through economic superiority and advancement. The narrow exclusivity of this position renders it invalid. Economic advancement and superiority do not equate to manhood or functional masculinity. Conversely, the absence of economic prominence does not render a man worthless or powerless.

Our goals for our sons included their focus on the perfect union of the spiritual, intellectual and physical components of the self. This primary goal formed the foundation for our approach to the rite of passage. We developed our bibliography with an eye to the spiritual and intellectual components. This is not a reflection of an indictment or dismissal of the physical component or our desire to relegate less attention to it. On the contrary, we recognize the impact of the physical on the creation and maintenance of balance and unity. Nevertheless the physical, especially as manifested in the lives of Black male children and adolescents, receives unquestioned dominance, approval and recognition in the natural, material world they inhabit. As a result we felt our sons were less in need of our encouragement, support, and direction in that realm.

We explored, examined and articulated first to one another and then to our sons our hopes, expectations and goals for them as African-American men. We forced ourselves to move beyond the immediate, beyond the current physical, material, and academic to imagine their lived futures. Yes we wanted them to complete high school and college. A graduate degree might be nice as well. We wanted them to find meaningful work with a living wage and of course we wanted them to marry spiritually and intellectually enlightened African or African-American women. However, we also wanted them to have a clear and conscious sense of commitment and responsibility to God, their community, and people of the African diaspora, wherever they may dwell in the global village. We knew the first set of goals would be repeated and supported by us and others involved in Charles' and Damon's lives. We wanted to articulate for ourselves, for our sons, and for our community that we value the other goals as well.

Step Two: Participation

This is a critical and somewhat tricky step. It was important for us to try to convince our sons that they actually needed and in fact wanted to devote approximately eight to nine months of their lives to intense, rigorous, academic, intellectual and spiritual work. We were not successful. They did not want to become involved in that level of work and effort. Essentially we clarified the process for them, what it would entail, what would be expected of them, and the level of support and assistance they could anticipate from us. While they were far from wildly enthusiastic, they did comply.

Our sons are fifth generation members of The Church of Christ of the Apostolic Faith. Although our church did not have a history of rite of passage ceremonies, our Pastor, Bishop Eugene Lundy, MD, readily and enthusiastically agreed to support us and our sons in this endeavor. We were able to schedule time with him on a monthly basis to review Charles' and Damon's essays on specific scriptures. Bishop Lundy performed the rite of passage ceremony at our church with great solemnity and his participation underscored the significance of the event for our sons.

We were also in the midst of our homeschooling "adventure" with all three of our sons. We were blessed with several graduate students at The Ohio State University who we hired to teach Biology, French and Math. Two of those graduate students, both PhD candidates, were Ghanaian scholars. Dr. Francis Cobbina (Mathematics) and Dr. Kwaku Gyasi (French) moved outside their disciplines and fully engaged Charles and Damon and their younger brother Evan in discussions of their readings of African authors. They also assisted Charles and Damon in the writing, pronunciation and presentation of their welcome in Asanti at the actual ceremony. Once more, the gracious and serious level of participation by these scholars highlighted the importance of the process for our sons.

On the day of the ceremony, after months of what must have seemed to Charles and Damon rather solitary labor, they were encouraged to by the presence of their extended family and community of friends. Members of our church choir gave up their Saturday morning to come and sing us through the process. Our Minister of Music, Brother Thommy Adams, prepared diligently for the ceremony, once more illuminating for our sons the depth of caring and commitment in community others had for them. The boys extended family, grandparents, great-grandmothers, aunts, uncles and cousins from near and far were there and actively participated. Numerous family friends, many of whom had known Charles and Damon from birth came and shared the passage with us. We all were moved by the accolades, congratulations, and sincere good wishes extended by so many different people. The love and commitment displayed by so many members of community conveyed the importance of the rite of passage in a deeply tangible way. It was a blessing to see our sons embraced and welcomed into the next phase of their lives.

The day concluded with active participation from Charles' and Damon's peers. That evening we had an "after party" complete with a DJ. At several stages throughout the preparation process, the promise of the party to come seemed the only thing that kept the boys going!

The myriad levels of participation in the preparation, presentation and celebration of the ceremony illustrated in countless ways the commitment of individuals, family, and community to the growth and development of these two young men. A reciprocal commitment from each of them was inevitable.

Step Three: Implementation

The implementation phase began with our clarification of precisely what we expected from Charles and Damon. We reviewed with them in detail the lengthy bibliography we had prepared. However we emphasized the amount of time they would have to read each week-generally 10 days. Even in the event of a 200 page book, a rarity in our bibliography, a 10-day window only required that they read 20 pages each day. We also stressed that we would be reading the same books and articles along with them. We wanted the boys to understand that the rite of passage was more than a ceremony, it was a culmination of much work, and a bridge to more work, responsibility and analysis as an adult.

Our active participation as parents, participants and scholars with them was the best example we could provide of the importance of lifelong learning. We promised to be available for critical discussions of the works they read and to engage them in the processing of the materials. These group discussions would occur prior to their required essays on the reading.

Our group discussions undoubtedly were more enlightening for us as parents than for Charles, Damon and Evan as children. We were amazed and impressed continually by their questions and comments. Their ability to draw connections between the readings also was exciting. The group discussions were designed to address questions about the reading assignments and to provide an opportunity to expand their thoughts on the works. Those group discussions seemed to help the boys sift through the information, synthesize and organize it which greatly helped the writing process.

The writing component of the preparation was the logical extension of the reading and discussion. Two objectives were to be met in each writing assignment. One objective focused on structure, form and grammar. The second objective centered on content and analysis. The essay requirements were rather simple and consistent for each reading. Each boy was required to provide an outline, 1st and 2nd drafts (at least) along with a final copy of a one-to-two page assessment of each work. We allocated five days for this writing process to be completed. As writing can sometimes be a painful labor process, we saw no point in allowing them to drag it out.

While time consuming, a process approach to writing helps establish a pattern of clarity in the actual writing. The outline was reviewed first to determine a logical flow and organization of their thoughts. Occasionally outlines had to be redone completely. More often outlines either
needed to be expanded or slightly reorganized. Once the outlines were returned, they began the first draft. When reviewing their drafts I handled issues of substance and CMadison whom I lovingly referred to as Mr. Computer/Mr. Grammar handled issues of form.

While the essay might begin with descriptive and/or normative analysis, we expected it to end with metaethical analysis. In other words, describing the work and attaching value to it is a fine beginning, however a conclusion, stating and explaining why value attaches is critical. For example, in writing about Dr. King's Letter from a Birmingham Jail, one might say it was a modern epistle, much like that written by the Apostle Paul from prison to the church at Corinth. This is a descriptive statement.

One might further state that the letter was good and espoused a value or virtue of justice. This is a normative statement. We wanted Charles and Damon to go further, to define and explain the concept of justice as a value, and why they thought it was good. That is metaethical analysis. As youngsters they were not always able to incorporate that level of analysis, however we felt it was important that they learn to strive to be comfortable with truly critical thinking.

Charles and Damon received their drafts back, loaded with what we hoped were constructive criticisms and helpful hints. Many times these comments were not well received by our sons. The information that an essay would in fact need to be rewritten, in toto, before a polished, final version would be ready, was not happy news. This was an understandably difficult process for Charles and Damon, and we were not without empathy. However, and this is critically important, it would have been the worst form of irresponsibility for us to accept mediocrity from them when excellence was not only required, but entirely possible.

Their desire to follow the path of least resistance was completely normal. Essentially their job as teenagers was to fight vigorously against anything other than playing, watching TV and hanging out with their friends. Our job was to create a space of tranquility and enable them to do the work assigned, to the best of their ability, in a spirit of commitment to excellence. And if that meant re-writing an essay three times, so be it.

Step Four: Continuation

The process of preparing for the rite of passage took Charles and Damon to a higher level of spiritual, intellectual and physical development. Within two months of the ceremony both boys received the gift of the Holy Ghost, evidenced by speaking in other tongues as the spirit of God gave utterance, as described in Acts 2:4. The spiritual insight they received through the process of preparation clearly touched each of them at a very deep level.

In the years between the completion of the process and their matriculation to college, both Charles and Damon displayed greater confidence in critical discussion and analysis of classical literature as well as popular writings in newspapers and magazines. Most significantly, the concept of community was no longer something to be explored in the abstract. And their commitment to that concept has continued to blossom and expand as the years unfold. The rite of passage ceremony crystallized in ways that words never could the importance of care, concern and commitment to community. Our challenge in continuation was to assist Charles and Damon in the growth of their commitment and responsibility.

Although they were no longer working with rigid deadlines, we still assigned significant amounts of reading to Charles and Damon and of course Evan. The readings continued to be global and with a decidedly African-American slant. The level of analysis they developed shone through in their discussions of what they read, whether they read DuBois or Dickens. Those same critical thinking skills have greatly facilitated their ability to identify and examine paradoxes in global history as well as current events. As part of the continuation of the rite of passage we encouraged Charles and Damon to examine critically not just challenges facing the world's population but to identify possible solutions as well.

Part II
The Program

The Church of Christ of the Apostolic Faith
May 15, 1993

Gye nyame
God alone

Christian Rite of Passage

Sankofa
Go back and retrieve it
Look to your past, forgotten heritage

Seekers of the Responsibilities of Manhood:
Kofi* Charles Madison Penn Nabrit
Kofi* Damon Princeton Penn Nabrit

Sons of Charles Nabrit and Paula Penn-Nabrit

*Kofi is a name from Ghana, West Africa. Kofi is the Ghanaian name for a male child born on Friday. Kofi means growth and development, our wish for Charles and Damon as they seek and accept the responsibilities of manhood.

Amanfo Akwaaba

Welcome People

Yede aseda ma Nyame, yen awofo yen nananom, yen abusua, yen akyerekyerefo ne yen namfonom.
Giving honor first to God, our parents, grandparents, godfather, family, teachers and friends

Yeda mo ase se mo ne yen redi yen awoda.
Yekasakyer e mo wo Ashanti kasa mu efiri se ewiase ahyese firi Afrika.
Thank you for being part of our celebration.
We speak to you in Ashanti in respect of the African ancestors of all humanity.

Mfoni a ewo mo nkrataa no so kyere yen dee se yehunu wo yen asetena mu.
SANKOFA-wo ante a san kotie.
GYE NYAME-Nyame a onwu da.
Ono na okuta tumi ene ahooden wo no.
The symbols on the program show what is good to know for our future as men.
SANKOFA-Go back and retrieve it.
Look to your past forgotten heritage.
GYE NYAME-God alone.
Symbol of the immortality, power and infallibility of God, with power over life and death.

Mo mmo mpaee ma yen emmere a yereye yen asede tese mmarima.
Pray for us as we seek the responsibilities of manhood.

Order of Service

Call to Devotion and Worship
Welcome and Recognition of Visitors

Choir Selection, *This is a Holy Place*
Responsive Reading, Acts 2:1-47
Recitation of Our History: Charles and Damon

Choir Selection, *I Know the Lord Has Laid His Hand on Me*
Responsive Reading, John 16:32-33
The Challenge of Our Present: Damon and Charles

Choir Selection, *Praise the Lord (He's Done Marvelous Things)*
Responsive Reading, Matthew 25:31-40
Commitment to Our Future: Charles and Damon

Choir Selection, *It Won't Be Long*
Responsive Reading, Revelation 21:3-7
Audience and Choir, *Lift Every Voice and Sing*
Responsive Reading, Psalms 23

Commitment and Pledge: Pastor, Father and Sons

Final Speeches: Charles and Damon
Choir Selection, *I'm Going Through*
Responsive Reading, Romans 12: 1-21

Ancestors and People of Influence
Responsive Readings, Proverbs 4:1-13; Matthew 5:1-12; Psalms 1:1-6;
Matthew 22:34-40; 1 Corinthians 13: 1-13.

Closing Comments and Benediction: Bishop Lundy
Choir Selection, *Hallelujah, The Lord Our God Reigns*

Responsive Reading
Acts 2

1 And when the day of Pentecost was fully come, they were all with one accord in one place.

2 And suddenly there came a sound from heaven as of a rushing mighty wind, and it filled all the house where they were sitting.

3 And there appeared unto them cloven tongues like as of fire, and it sat upon each of them.

4 And they were all filled with the Holy Ghost, and began to speak with other tongues, as the Spirit gave them utterance.

5 And there were dwelling at Jerusalem Jews, devout men, out of every nation under heaven.

6 Now when this was noised abroad, the multitude came together, and were confounded, because that every man heard them speak in his own language.

7 And they were all amazed and marvelled, saying one to another, Behold, are not all these which speak Galilaeans?

8 And how hear we every man in our own tongue, wherein we were born?

9 Parthians, and Medes, and Elamites, and the dwellers in Mesopotamia, and in Judaea, and Cappadocia, in Pontus, and Asia,

10 Phrygia, and Pamphylia, in Egypt, and in the parts of Libya about Cyrene, and strangers of Rome, Jews and proselytes,

11 Cretes and Arabians, we do hear them speak in our tongues the

wonderful works of God.

12 And they were all amazed, and were in doubt, saying one to another, What meaneth this?

13 Others mocking said, These men are full of new wine.

14 But Peter, standing up with the eleven, lifted up his voice, and said unto them, Ye men of Judaea, and all ye that dwell at Jerusalem, be this known unto you, and hearken to my words:

15 For these are not drunken, as ye suppose, seeing it is but the third hour of the day.

16 But this is that which was spoken by the prophet Joel;

17 And it shall come to pass in the last days, saith God, I will pour out of my Spirit upon all flesh: and your sons and your daughters shall prophesy, and your young men shall see visions, and your old men shall dream dreams:

18 And on my servants and on my handmaidens I will pour out in those days of my Spirit; and they shall prophesy:

19 And I will shew wonders in heaven above, and signs in the earth beneath; blood, and fire, and vapour of smoke:

20 The sun shall be turned into darkness, and the moon into blood, before the great and notable day of the Lord come:

21 And it shall come to pass, that whosoever shall call on the name of the Lord shall be saved.

22 Ye men of Israel, hear these words; Jesus of Nazareth, a man approved of

God among you by miracles and wonders and signs, which God did by him in the midst of you, as ye yourselves also know:

23 Him, being delivered by the determinate counsel and foreknowledge of God, ye have taken, and by wicked hands have crucified and slain:

24 Whom God hath raised up, having loosed the pains of death: because it was not possible that he should be holden of it.

25 For David speaketh concerning him, I foresaw the Lord always before my face, for he is on my right hand, that I should not be moved:

26 Therefore did my heart rejoice, and my tongue was glad; moreover also my flesh shall rest in hope:

27 Because thou wilt not leave my soul in hell, neither wilt thou suffer thine Holy One to see corruption.

28 Thou hast made known to me the ways of life; thou shalt make me full of joy with thy countenance.

29 Men and brethren, let me freely speak unto you of the patriarch David, that he is both dead and buried, and his sepulchre is with us unto this day.

30 Therefore being a prophet, and knowing that God had sworn with an oath to him, that of the fruit of his loins, according to the flesh, he would raise up Christ to sit on his throne;

31 He seeing this before spake of the resurrection of Christ, that his soul was not left in hell, neither his flesh did see corruption.

32 This Jesus hath God raised up, whereof we all are witnesses.

33 **Therefore being by the right hand of God exalted, and having received of the Father the promise of the Holy Ghost, he hath shed forth this, which ye now see and hear.**

34 For David is not ascended into the heavens: but he saith himself, The Lord said unto my Lord, Sit thou on my right hand,

35 Until I make thy foes thy footstool.
36 Therefore let all the house of Israel know assuredly, that God hath made the same Jesus, whom ye have crucified, both Lord and Christ.

37 Now when they heard this, they were pricked in their heart, and said unto Peter and to the rest of the apostles, Men and brethren, what shall we do?

38 Then Peter said unto them, Repent, and be baptized every one of you in the name of Jesus Christ for the remission of sins, and ye shall receive the gift of the Holy Ghost.

39 For the promise is unto you, and to your children, and to all that are afar off, even as many as the Lord our God shall call.

40 And with many other words did he testify and exhort, saying, Save yourselves from this untoward generation.

41 Then they that gladly received his word were baptized: and the same day there were added unto them about three thousand souls.

42 And they continued stedfastly in the apostles' doctrine and fellowship, and in breaking of bread, and in prayers.

43 And fear came upon every soul: and many wonders and signs were done by the apostles.

44 And all that believed were together, and had all things common;

45 And sold their possessions and goods, and parted them to all men, as every man had need.

46 And they, continuing daily with one accord in the temple, and breaking bread from house to house, did eat their meat with gladness and singleness of heart,

47 Praising God, and having favour with all the people. And the Lord added to the church daily such as should be saved.

The Past

by Charles Madison Penn Nabrit

The past of the Black man has been long, hard, and trying. Our oppressors tried, and in some instances succeeded in making us ashamed of our heritage, leaders, and accomplishments. In many cases where the oppressors have succeeded their dominance was achieved and maintained by the power given to them by others.

The oppressors tried to systematically eliminate the existence and reduce the impact of black peoples throughout the world. Still, our influence has been felt throughout the world. Some might say the very presence of a person influences their environment. I think that is true. But I also think that African-Americans have done more than that. We have reshaped the constitutional foundation of the United States through legislation that has benefitted not only people of color, women and people with varied religious beliefs. From physical and architectural influences to cultural and intangible spiritual influences, the presence of African peoples has been felt throughout the history of the world.

In terms of recent history, one of the most significant things that has happened to Black people was the diaspora of African peoples through the institution of slavery. Diaspora, unlike other migratory processes is an unwilling movement of a people. Other groups have also experienced diasporas, such as Jews and Native Americans. However in the case of Africans the diaspora was especially hard because we were taken to places where we did not know the language, separated from our tribesmen and families, and denied access to our history. This was tragic because all people are connected and the history of one group will always impact the others.

In "Genes, People and Languages" an article by Stanford Professor Luigi Luca Cavalli-Sforzo, in the November 1991 issue of Scientific American, the history of Black people is shown as the history of all people. The professor talked about his 12-year study on the migrations of humanity. He traced genetic differences backwards through the division and migration of groups of people. He showed that the first migration of humanity emerged from Africa about 150 thousand years ago. This first migratory group traveled the Isthmus of Suez into Asia. The next migration was from Asia to Europe, then simultaneously to Australia and the Americas across the Bering Straits. This study showed the links between the migrations of people and their linguistic and cultural development. His conclusion was that all life began in and around central and sub-saharan Africa. So the history of Black people is the history of all people and we should all know our history and learn from it.

The Past
by Damon Princeton Penn Nabrit

Black people, or people of African descent, have seen good times and bad times. We have been the object of fear and domination by others. Sometimes we have given up our power to others, not physically, but spiritually, and in our attempts to assimilate into the dominant culture. Other ethnic groups and groups of people of color have done many of the same things. I think that it really doesn't make a value difference what your racial identity is because it is never bad to be what God made you. What is bad or wrong is to try to be something or someone you are not because you are ashamed of what you are. One does not have to denigrate other ethnic groups to feel good about oneself.

Black people have had great influence not just in one place, but all over the world. Here in the Americas we have changed whole governments in ways that have benefited everyone. The presence of a people doesn't guarantee that they will have an influence in that place, rather it is the actions of that people that create an influence. The impact and influence of people of African descent is important for all people because all people originated in Africa.

In "Genes, People and Languages" an article by Professor Luigi Luca Cavalli-Storza in the November 1991 issue of Scientific American, the origin of humanity is traced to one single African woman. The study used two independent scientific studies to prove the hypothesis. The first female appeared on the earth in Africa between 150 to 200 thousand years ago. This conclusion is the result of genetic tracking. The mitochondrial gene which powers DNA is passed by the mother. The research tracked that gene backwards to its point of origin in Africa. Although the Professor believes there may have been other women in Africa about the same time, he thinks their mitochondrial trails became extinct. I disagree. I believe there was one original woman, Eve, as described in Genesis. The Professor is an evolutionist while I am a creationist. We do agree however on the location of the origins of humanity.

The Doctor followed genetic splits to determine the major migrations from Africa. The first occurred about 100 thousand years ago, through the Isthmus of Suez, into Asia. The second occurred about 50 thousand years ago into Europe, and the final migration occurred between 35 and 40 thousand years ago as people moved into Australia and the Americas across the Bering Straits.

Along with these genetic changes and migrations, linguistic and cultural alterations happened. Genetic change is slow and occurs through the intermingling of people while linguistic and cultural changes occur more rapidly when people are conquered and oppressed. That is one reason language cannot be determined from race because language can change rapidly r slowly depending on the social, cultural, and political circumstances of the people.

A good example of this was the loss of language and culture by people of African descent due to the diaspora. The diaspora was not a voluntary migration and so the people who were transported as slaves to Europe, the West Indies and all the Americas, were not able to maintain their language or culture.

This history of Black people is important to me, not just because I am Black, but because I am a person and this is the history of us all.

Choir Selection
I Know The Lord Has Laid His Hand On Me

Responsive Reading
John 16: 32-33

32. Behold, the hour cometh, yea, is now come, that ye shall be scattered, every man to his own, and shall leave me alone: and yet I am not alone, because the Father is with me.

33. These things I have spoken unto you, that in me ye might have peace. In the world ye shall have tribulation: but be of good cheer; I have overcome the world.

The Challenge of Our Present
by Damon Princeton Penn Nabrit

Romans Chapter 12 provides a good basis for my assessment of the present and my role as an African-American man in it. Romans Chapter 12 has basically three parts to it. The first section is telling me that I am a living sacrifice to God. The second tells me to serve God with spiritual gifts and the third section tells me to behave as a Christian. A big portion of my obligation in the present is to find out what my spiritual gifts are so I can use them to serve God.

In "Letter from a Birmingham Jail" an excerpt from Dr. Martin Luther King, Jr.'s book <u>Why We Can't Wait</u>, Dr. King speaks to the difficulty of finding and using spiritual gifts. I think Dr. King's letter speaks to everyone who really thinks. Dr. King was doing what he thought was right, he was using his spiritual gift of ministry to bring about social justice. Many of his peers disagreed with him. These ministers were calling his activities "unwise and untimely.: They were wrong. I do not think they had a valid spiritual reason to criticize Dr. King because I do not think Jesus was offended by his sacrifice for others. I think many of them were supporting the status quo and the dominant culture unconsciously, even if it meant going against the teachings of Christ. Unfortunately many ministers of many faiths become confused and try to strengthen their material rather than spiritual positions.

Dr. King said he was in Birmingham because "injustice is here." I do not think he saw or cared about the fame he received as a result of his work. He had discovered his spiritual gift and was using it. He knew that allowing his spiritual gifts to manifest would benefit everyone. I think that with the guidance of Jesus, I can, in my present, discover my spiritual gifts and use them for my people, my country, and the global community of which I am a member.

The Present
by Charles Madison Penn Nabrit

In Romans 12 God makes clear that everyone and everything has a place and a reason for being here on Earth. For example, God made man to have dominion over beasts. This is why bees give us honey and cross pollinate flowers and trees, which, in turn, give us medicine, fruit, and shade. We do our part by protecting and not destroying the environment. Having dominion does not mean we have the right to destroy or abuse other living things. The reason for this relationship and responsibility is because God made man in His own image. Part of the challenge of my present is to discover my place and reason for being here on Earth.

It is the same in the church body today. The pastor has dominion over the church. And, as in nature, he, the pastor, cannot keep the word and house of God functioning without the help of other members in the church so the word of God can reach outside the church. In the church the pastor must be able to stay humble and on the paths of righteousness. He must also keep the members of the church living in the same manner. The pastor must also not use his authority to persecute and gain vengeance on others. The pastor has to set an example for the church to follow by praying for those who persecute him, praying fervently, and not being slothful in business for the church.

All of this is part of the responsibility of the pastor to be an example to others. Part of my responsibility in my present is to follow that example and be a contributing member of my church and to treat people with kindness and understanding even when they make me mad.

Choir Selection
Praise the Lord, He's Done Marvelous Things

Responsive Reading
Matthew 25: 31-40

31. When the Son of man shall come in his glory, and all the holy angels with him, then shall he sit upon the throne of his glory:

32 And before him shall be gathered all nations: and he shall separate them one from another, as a shepherd divideth his sheep from the goats:

33 And he shall set the sheep on his right hand, but the goats on the left.

34 Then shall the King say unto them on his right hand, Come, ye blessed of my Father, inherit the kingdom prepared for you from the foundation of the world:

35 For I was an hungred, and ye gave me meat: I was thirsty, and ye gave me drink: I was a stranger, and ye took me in:

36 Naked, and ye clothed me: I was sick, and ye visited me: I was in prison, and ye came unto me.

37 Then shall the righteous answer him, saying, Lord, when saw we thee an hungred, and fed thee? or thirsty, and gave thee drink?

38 When saw we thee a stranger, and took thee in? or naked, and clothed thee?

39 Or when saw we thee sick, or in prison, and came unto thee?

40 And the King shall answer and say unto them, Verily I say unto you, Inasmuch as ye have done it unto one of the least of these my brethren, ye have done it unto me.

Commitment to Our Future
by Charles Madison Penn Nabrit

In Chapter Five, "Letter from a Birmingham Jail" in Dr. Martin Luther King, Jr.'s book, <u>Why We Can't Wait</u>, I found some insights for my future. One of the most compelling was asking why there was, and if there still is, a need for non-violent demonstrations. Although some of the questions seems dated and of little help in today's world, others have a useful meaning even in today's changing world.

Dr. King questioned the moral implications and obligations of all people and especially Black people. Some of those obligations and implications have to do with our sense of community. Dr. King recognized Black people's need to live in community. The communal connection we feel towards one another has created insecurity within the dominant culture. This insecurity operates on a level that is so discreet and sophisticated that it has become largely accepted and part of the status quo.

Stephen Biko, a Black South African martyr and opponent of apartheid, also questioned the moral implications and obligations of Black people. In <u>I Write What I Like</u>, Mr. Biko speaks of black consciousness as a moral obligation. I think Mr. Biko is trying to warn the reader about the absence of "black consciousness." Black consciousness is not a trivial subject. By the absence of consciousness, the younger generation is confused and the stage is set for another generation of oppression. I also think that oppression should have been stopped earlier when it wasn't as great and the technology supporting it wasn't so strong. I think oppression is the destruction of heritage, religion, and self-esteem. Some of the warning to the reader is about the people who have given in to the oppression of so many years and who may be on the brink of a violent outbreak. Mr. Biko is warning about those who have given in, have been broken and have become a shell of a person. He is telling the reader that by trying to break the spirit of Black Africans, the oppressor has over the years robbed almost all Blacks of their heritage. Others have been oppressed to the end of their endurance and believe that violence is the only way. I think that Stephen Biko is telling the reader that neither is right and that only non-violent negotiations are the way to equality in Africa and elsewhere.

Oppressing others prevents spiritual growth. Oppressors may build massive structures and improve technology, but they cannot grow materially either, at least not indefinitely. At first it might seem as if they are growing materially, but in the end their economy and power structure will collapse. My goal in the future as an African-American man is to be fully conscious; conscious of who I am and what my responsibilities are to God, my church, my people, my community and my family.

The Future
by Damon Princeton Penn Nabrit

The greatest gift God can give is love. "Love never fails." Those words and insights provided in I Corinthians 13 should be used to shape our future. There are so many different gifts, but love is the greatest gift of all. What is love you say? Well love is different for every person. Some people think that it is purely physical while others think that it is charity, or concern for others. The dictionary says love is a warm and tender liking, deep feeling of fondness and friendship, great affection or devotion.

I think that love can only come from the heart and soul, and that everyone is born with the power and ability to love and receive love in the right way. I also think that one has to have a deep desire for something or someone before one can honestly say that one loves it. A person can have everything their heart desires, but without love, they are nothing at all. The Scriptures say that God so loved the world that He gave His only begotten son, that whosoever believeth in Him should not perish but have everlasting life. 1 John 3:16. That means God loved us so much that He gave His only son, just so we could repent of our sins, be baptized, and receive the gift of the Holy Ghost, and live forever in God's arms.

I think part of the reason God could love so completely was because He was God and He knew who He ws. In other words, I think He knew Himself and so He was able to love all humanity. In order for me to love completely I must know and love myself, I must become conscious of myself. In Stephen Biko's book, <u>I Write What I Like</u>, he speaks about"black consciousness." I think Black consciousness as Mr. Biko puts it, means that Black people as a whole, in the United States of America and elsewhere, have been unconscious for a long time. Many of us have been unconscious of our past as well as our potential. Black consciousness means becoming fully conscious of who we are, where we have been, what our function is in the world.

In <u>The History of the Negro</u> by Carter G. Woodson, the father of African and African-American studies, Dr. Woodson indicates the importance of knowing oneself before one can be fully functioning. Some Black people, like W.E.B.DuBois, Marcus Garvey, and Franz Fanon have been somewhat conscious, but many have been caught in the trap of assimilation, trying to become like the dominant culture. This is not an act of self love. The Scriptures say "to love thy neighbor as thyself." To do that I must first know and then love myself. That is my challenge for the future, to more fully know and love myself as an African-American man so that I can show that love in my dealings with everyone else.

Choir Selection
It Won't Be Long

Responsive Reading
Revelation 21: 3-7

3 And I heard a great voice out of heaven saying, Behold, the tabernacle of God is with men, and he will dwell with them, and they shall be his people, and God himself shall be with them, and be their God.

4 And God shall wipe away all tears from their eyes; and there shall be no more death, neither sorrow, nor crying, neither shall there be any more pain: for the former things are passed away.

5 And he that sat upon the throne said, Behold, I make all things new. And he said unto me, Write: for these words are true and faithful.

6 And he said unto me, It is done. I am Alpha and Omega, the beginning and the end. I will give unto him that is athirst of the fountain of the water of life freely.

7 He that overcometh shall inherit all things; and I will be his God, and he shall be my son.

Choir and Audience Selection
Lift Every Voice and Sing
The Negro National Anthem by James Weldon Johnson

Lift every voice and sing,
Till earth and heaven ring,
Ring with the harmonies of Liberty;
Let our rejoicing rise
High as the list'ning skies,
Let it resound loud as the rolling sea.
Sing a song full of the faith that the dark past has taught us,
Sing a song full of the hope that the present has brought us;
Facing the rising sun of our new day begun,
Let us march on till victory is won.

Stony the road we trod,
Bitter the chast'ning rod,
Felt in the days when hope unborn had died;
Yet with a steady beat,
Have not our weary feet
Come to the place for which our fathers sighed?
We have come over a way that with tears has been watered.
We have come, treading our path through the blood of the slaughtered,
Out from the gloomy past,
Till now we stand at last
Where the white gleam of our bright star is cast.

God of our weary years,
God of our silent tears,
Thou who hast brought us thus far on the way;
Thou who hast by Thy might,
Led us into the light,
Keep us forever in the path, we pray.
Lest our feet stray from the places, our God, where we met Thee,
Lest our hearts, drunk with the wine of the world, we forget Thee;
Shadowed beneath Thy hand,
May we forever stand,
True to our God,
True to our native land.

Responsive Reading
Psalms 23

1 The Lord is my shepherd; I shall not want.

2 He maketh me to lie down in green pastures: he leadeth me beside the still waters.

3 He restoreth my soul: he leadeth me in the paths of righteousness for his name's sake.

4 Yea, though I walk through the valley of the shadow of death, I will fear no evil: for thou art with me; thy rod and thy staff they comfort me.

5 Thou preparest a table before me in the presence of mine enemies: thou anointest my head with oil; my cup runneth over.

6 Surely goodness and mercy shall follow me all the days of my life: and I will dwell in the house of the Lord for ever.

Commitment and Pledge
Pastor, Father, and Sons

Final Speech
By Charles Madison Penn Nabrit

In the past several weeks I have done extensive research about the past. The past of my family, my church, the past of Black people of African descent, and the past of humanity. I have learned and discovered more than I could have ever imagined about the strength and struggle of my brothers and sisters as well as our ancestors.

In preparing for this program I have also come to enjoy several things I once detested doing, such as writing essays on just about everything I read. I used to think that my mother was just exaggerating when she said I would feel good when I saw the results of writing and rewriting the same essay. Now I realize she was telling me the truth because I can see the difference in my writing and my thinking. I have started to enjoy family talks with my mother and father about current issues, events and world politics, something I used to hate. Because of this experience I have begun to think seriously and critically about my life and what I believe.

I believe my spiritual existence is critical. I believe Jesus is God and that only He has power over life and death and that He conquered Satan, sin, death, and the grave and still came back on the third day. I believe in the apostolic faith and in being baptized in water and spirit. I believe God made man in His own image and that all life began in Africa. I am glad I know who I am, where I come from, and what I believe.

At this time I would like to thank first God and then my mother because without her standing over us all the time I don't think any of this would have been possible. I would also like to thank my father for all the books he got for us and reading the really difficult ones with us. I would also like to thank Elder Lundy for being with us so much and talking to us seriously and not like we were stupid. I would also like to thank all our friends in the Mass Choir, the musicians, and especially Brother Adams for being so nice to me. I would like to especially thank Aunt Cecilia and my unofficial Aunt Louise for coming all the way from Nashville. Finally, I would like to thank all my other family and friends from near and far who came out this early on Saturday and missed cutting the grass or watching cartoons.

Final Speech
by Damon Princeton Penn Nabrit

I think I have really grown as a result of this experience. My writing has improved a great deal. I find that I can write more comfortably and so I write more. It is easier for me to organize my thoughts and so the quality of my work has improved too. I have also had to develop better time-management skills throughout this experience. My parents would not let me skip any of my other academic work or projects because of this activity. I had lots and lots of work to do on my essays because we ad to write them over several times. We also had to learn our welcome in Asanti.

I have also learned more about what it is to be a Black man in this society. I hope other Christian boys who are going out into manhood will have the same opportunities that Charles and I have had.

I would like to thank first God, who has shown me the way to go and my parents for helping me through this. I would also like to thank Elder Lundy for spending so much time with us and reading all our essays and Kwaku and Francis for teaching us Ashanti along with French and Math, and Brother Adams for being so thoughtful to my whole family. I especially want to thank Evan for being such a great little brother, even when Charles and I were getting a lot of attention.

Choir Selection
I'm Going Through

Responsive Reading
Romans 12

1 I beseech you therefore, brethren, by the mercies of God, that ye present your bodies a living sacrifice, holy, acceptable unto God, which is your reasonable service.

2 And be not conformed to this world: but be ye transformed by the renewing of your mind, that ye may prove what is that good, and acceptable, and perfect, will of God.

3 For I say, through the grace given unto me, to every man that is among you, not to think of himself more highly than he ought to think; but to think soberly, according as God hath dealt to every man the measure of faith.

4 For as we have many members in one body, and all members have not the

same office:

5 So we, being many, are one body in Christ, and every one members one of another.

6 Having then gifts differing according to the grace that is given to us, whether prophecy, let us prophesy according to the proportion of faith;

7 Or ministry, let us wait on our ministering: or he that teacheth, on teaching;

8 Or he that exhorteth, on exhortation: he that giveth, let him do it with simplicity; he that ruleth, with diligence; he that sheweth mercy, with cheerfulness.

9 Let love be without dissimulation. Abhor that which is evil; cleave to that which is good.

10 Be kindly affectioned one to another with brotherly love; in honour preferring one another;

11 Not slothful in business; fervent in spirit; serving the Lord;

12 Rejoicing in hope; patient in tribulation; continuing instant in prayer;

13 Distributing to the necessity of saints; given to hospitality.

14 Bless them which persecute you: bless, and curse not.

15 Rejoice with them that do rejoice, and weep with them that weep.

16 Be of the same mind one toward another. Mind not high things, but condescend to men of low estate. Be not wise in your own conceits.

17 Recompense to no man evil for evil. Provide things honest in the sight of all men.

18 If it be possible, as much as lieth in you, live peaceably with all men.

19 Dearly beloved, avenge not yourselves, but rather give place unto wrath: for it is written, Vengeance is mine; I will repay, saith the Lord.

20 Therefore if thine enemy hunger, feed him; if he thirst, give him drink: for in so doing thou shalt heap coals of fire on his head.

21 Be not overcome of evil, but overcome evil with good.

Ancestors and People of Influence
Acknowledgement and Testimony*

Parents

Paternal Grandparents
Maternal Grandparents

Paternal Great-Grandmother
Maternal Great-Grandmother

Aunts and Uncles
Great Aunts and Great Uncles

Godfather

Teachers

*Each of the ancestors and people of influence who attended the ceremony prepared and presented their own testimony, encouragement and acknowledgement to Charles and Damon. The individual comments were profoundly moving, and while each were unique, the common bond of sincere caring and commitment was overwhelming.

Let All Men Connected by the Blood of Family to these Seeking Manhood Stand and Read Responsively

Proverbs 4:1-13

1 Hear, ye children, the instruction of a father, and attend to know understanding.

2 For I give you good doctrine, forsake ye not my law.

3 For I was my father's son, tender and only beloved in the sight of my mother.

4 He taught me also, and said unto me, Let thine heart retain my words: keep my commandments, and live.

5 Get wisdom, get understanding: forget it not; neither decline from the words of my mouth.

6 Forsake her not, and she shall preserve thee: love her, and she shall keep thee.

7 Wisdom is the principal thing; therefore get wisdom: and with all thy getting get understanding.

8 Exalt her, and she shall promote thee: she shall bring thee to honour, when thou dost embrace her.

9 She shall give to thine head an ornament of grace: a crown of glory

shall she deliver to thee.

10 Hear, O my son, and receive my sayings; and the years of thy life shall be many.

11 I have taught thee in the way of wisdom; I have led thee in right paths.

12 When thou goest, thy steps shall not be straitened; and when thou runnest, thou shalt not stumble.

13 Take fast hold of instruction; let her not go: keep her; for she is thy life.

Let All Women Connected by the Blood of Family to these Seeking Manhood Stand and Read Responsively

Matthew 5:1-12

1 And seeing the multitudes, he went up into a mountain: and when he was set, his disciples came unto him:

2 And he opened his mouth, and taught them, saying,

3 Blessed are the poor in spirit: for theirs is the kingdom of heaven.

4 Blessed are they that mourn: for they shall be comforted.

5 Blessed are the meek: for they shall inherit the earth.

6 Blessed are they which do hunger and thirst after righteousness: for they shall be filled.

7 Blessed are the merciful: for they shall obtain mercy.

8 Blessed are the pure in heart: for they shall see God.

9 Blessed are the peacemakers: for they shall be called the children of God.

10 Blessed are they which are persecuted for righteousness' sake: for theirs is the kingdom of heaven.

11 Blessed are ye, when men shall revile you, and persecute you, and shall say all manner of evil against you falsely, for my sake.

12 Rejoice, and be exceeding glad: for great is your reward in heaven: for so persecuted they the prophets which were before you.

Let All Men Connected by the Blood of Jesus to these Seeking Manhood Stand and Read Responsively

Psalms 1:1-6

1 Blessed is the man that walketh not in the counsel of the ungodly, nor standeth in the way of sinners, nor sitteth in the seat of the scornful.

2 But his delight is in the law of the Lord; and in his law doth he meditate day and night.

3 And he shall be like a tree planted by the rivers of water, that bringeth forth his fruit in his season; his leaf also shall not wither; and whatsoever he doeth shall prosper.

4 The ungodly are not so: but are like the chaff which the wind driveth away.

5 Therefore the ungodly shall not stand in the judgment, nor sinners in the congregation of the righteous.

6 For the Lord knoweth the way of the righteous: but the way of the ungodly shall perish.

Let All Women Connected by the Blood of Jesus to these Seeking Manhood Stand and Read Responsively

Matthew 22: 34-40

34 But when the Pharisees had heard that he had put the Sadducees to silence, they were gathered together.

35 Then one of them, which was a lawyer, asked him a question, tempting him, and saying,

36 Master, which is the great commandment in the law?

37 Jesus said unto him, Thou shalt love the Lord thy God with all thy heart, and with all thy soul, and with all thy mind.

38 This is the first and great commandment.

39 And the second is like unto it, Thou shalt love thy neighbour as thyself.

40 On these two commandments hang all the law and the prophets.

Let All People Connected by the Ancestors, the Love of Humanity, and Belief in the Power of Prayer and Meditation to these Seeking Manhood Stand and Read Responsively

1 Corinthians 13

1 Though I speak with the tongues of men and of angels, and have not charity, I am become as sounding brass, or a tinkling cymbal.

2 And though I have the gift of prophecy, and understand all mysteries, and all knowledge; and though I have all faith, so that I could remove mountains, and have not charity, I am nothing.

3 And though I bestow all my goods to feed the poor, and though I give my body to be burned, and have not charity, it profiteth me nothing.

4 Charity suffereth long, and is kind; charity envieth not; charity vaunteth not itself, is not puffed up,

5 Doth not behave itself unseemly, seeketh not her own, is not easily provoked, thinketh no evil;

6 Rejoiceth not in iniquity, but rejoiceth in the truth;

7 Beareth all things, believeth all things, hopeth all things, endureth all things.

8 Charity never faileth: but whether there be prophecies, they shall fail; whether there be tongues, they shall cease; whether there be knowledge, it shall vanish away.

9 For we know in part, and we prophesy in part.

10 But when that which is perfect is come, then that which is in part shall be done away.

11 When I was a child, I spake as a child, I understood as a child, I thought as a child: but when I became a man, I put away childish things.

12 For now we see through a glass, darkly; but then face to face: now I know in part; but then shall I know even as also I am known.

13 And now abideth faith, hope, charity, these three; but the greatest of these is charity.

Closing

Elder Lundy: *Charles and Damon, we welcome you to the honored realm, challenges, and responsibilities of Black manhood.*

Benediction
by Elder Lundy

Choir Selection
Hallelujah, The Lord Our God Reigns

Reception in the Fellowship Hall

Bibliography and References

for Charles and Damon

Bell, Derrick, <u>And We are Not Saved</u>. Basic Books, Inc., 1987.

Bell, Derrick, <u>Faces at the Bottom of the Well</u>, Basic Books, Inc., 1992.

Biko, Steve, <u>I Write What I Like</u>. Harper & Row, New York, 1978.

DuBois, W.E.B., <u>The Souls of Black Folk</u>. Bantam Books, New York, 1989.

James, George G.M., <u>Stolen Legacy</u>. The African Publication Society, 1980.

King, Martin Luther, <u>Why We Can't Wait</u>. The New American Library, New York, 1964.

Lemelle, Sid, <u>Pan-Africanism for Beginners</u>. Writers and Readers Publishing, Inc., 1992.

Rogers, J.A., <u>Sex and Race</u>. 1945

Williams, Eric, <u>Capitalism & Slavery</u>. Capricorn Books, New York, 1966.

Woodson, Carter Godwin, <u>The Negro in our History</u>. The Associated Publishers, Inc., Washington, D.C., 1941.

Woodson, Carter Godwin, <u>The Mis-Education of the Negro</u>. AMS Press, NY, NY, 1977.

<u>African Proverbs</u>, compiled by Leslau, Charlotte and Wolf. Peter Pauper Press, Inc., White Plains, New York, 1985.

<u>The African Diaspora, Interpretive Essays</u>, ed. By Kilson, Martin L. and Rotberg, Robert I. Harvard University Press, Cambridge, Massachusetts, 1976.

<u>The Holy Bible</u>, The King James Version.

The Horizon History of Africa, American Heritage Publishing Co., Inc., NY, NY, 1971.

The Langston Hughes Reader, George Braziller, Inc., NY, NY, 1971.

Additional Bibliography

for

Parents

Hacker, Andrew, Two Nations, Black and White, Separate, Hostile, and Unequal. Ballantine Books, New York, 1992.

Hare, Ph.D., Nathan and Julia, Bringing the Black Boy to Manhood: The Passage. Black Think Tank, San Francisco, 1985.

Hill, Paul, J., Coming of Age, African American Male Rites-of-Passage. African American Images, Chicago, Illinois, 1992.

Back Cover

Rites of Passage ceremonies are not new, but they symbolize the beginning of a new life phase-the transition from childhood to adulthood. Many of our children today are confused about which group they belong in and what behaviors are appropriate.

<u>Sankofa: Look to Your Past Forgotten Heritage</u> speaks to the frequently ignored need for guidance, purpose, and encouragement for African-American youth. Paula Penn-Nabrit describes an easily adaptable approach to guiding African-American male adolescents through the process toward true, holistically healthy manhood.

Like Rites of Passage, <u>Sankofa</u> is not new. It was originally published in 1995. Charles and Damon, the 13 year-old participants in the rite of passage recounted are now holistically healthy, 37 year-old African-American men. The process proved impactful enough in their lives to warrant a reissue of the book. ***#StillTimely***